Be a History Detective

Victorian Factory

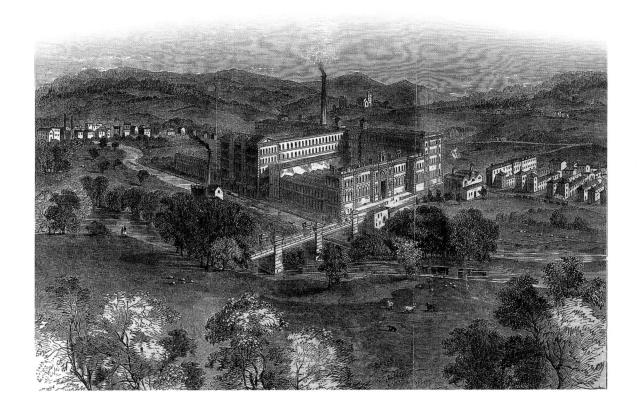

Susie Brooks

WAYLAND

This book is a differentiated text version of
The History Detective Investigates Victorian Factory
by Colin Stott

This edition first published in 2009 by Wayland.

Wayland
Hachette Children's Books
338 Euston Road
London NW1 3BH

Wayland Australia
Level 17/207 Kent Street
Sydney NSW 2000

Commissioning Editor: Jennifer Sanderson
Designer: Elaine Wilkinson
Proofreader: Hayley Fairhead
Cartoon Artwork: Richard Hook
Picture research: Shelley Noronha

British Library Cataloguing in Publication Data:
 Brooks, Susie
 Victorian factory. - Differentiated ed. -
 (Be a history detective)
 1. Factories - Great Britain -
 History - 19th century -
 Juvenile literature 2. Great Britain -
 Social conditions -
 19th century - Juvenile literature
 I. Title II. Stott, Colin
 338.4'7670941'09034

ISBN: 978 0 7502 5707 7

Printed in China

Wayland is a division of Hachette Children's Books,
an Hachette UK Company.
www.hachette.co.uk

Picture acknowledgements:
The Publishers would like to thank the following for
permission to reproduce their pictures: Billie Love
Historical Collection 17 (top); The Bridgeman Art
Library 5, 7 (bottom), 8, 15, 26 (top and bottom);
Colmans of Norwich 10; Hulton Deutsch 23 (bottom);
Hulton Getty cover (right), 4 (top), 7 (top), 14 (top
and bottom), 16 (top), 25 (top), 28 and cover, 29
(bottom) and cover; Hodder Wayland Picture Library
6 (bottom), 13 (right), 21 (top), 24; Mansell 22 (top),
29; Mary Evans Picture Library 1 and cover, 4
(bottom) and cover, 6 (top), 9 (top and bottom), 11
(bottom), 12, 16 (bottom), 18, 19, 20, 21 (bottom) and
cover, 22 (bottom), 27; PRO 25 (bottom); Salford
Working Class Movement Library / Museum of
Labour, Manchester 11 (top); Wellcome Institute
Library 13 (top).

Note:
The website addresses included in this book were valid at
the time of going to press. However, because of the nature
of the Internet, it is possible that some addresses may have
changed, or sites may have changed or closed down since
publication. While the authors and Publishers regret any
inconvenience this may cause the readers, no responsibility
for any such changes can be accepted by either the author
or the Publishers.

Contents

Words in **bold** can be
found in the glossary.

The Victorian times

Queen Victoria ruled
Britain from 1837 until
1901. We call this period
the Victorian times.
Victorian Britain was
one of the most powerful
countries in the world.
It was also the place
where many great
ideas and inventions
were born.

▶ *Queen Victoria sits
at a spinning wheel
in 1857.*

▼ *Victorian women work in a
bicycle factory in Coventry.*

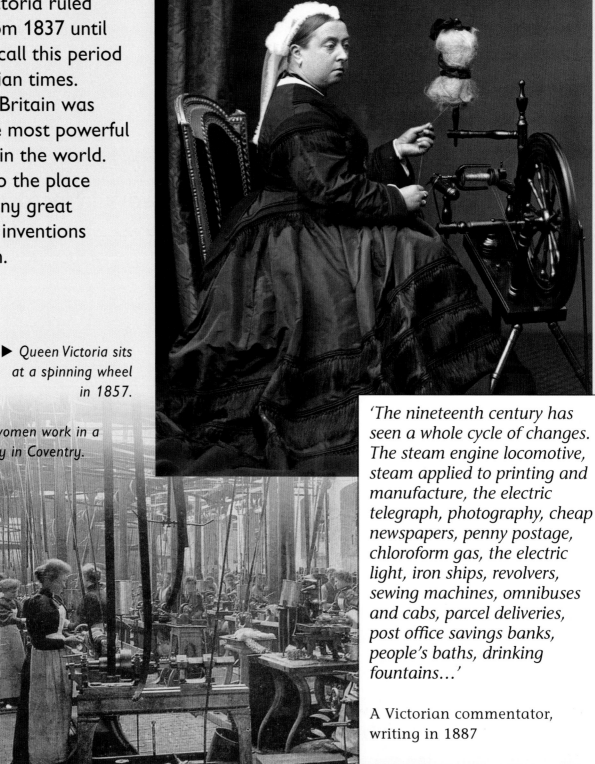

'The nineteenth century has
seen a whole cycle of changes.
The steam engine locomotive,
steam applied to printing and
manufacture, the electric
telegraph, photography, cheap
newspapers, penny postage,
chloroform gas, the electric
light, iron ships, revolvers,
sewing machines, omnibuses
and cabs, parcel deliveries,
post office savings banks,
people's baths, drinking
fountains…'

A Victorian commentator,
writing in 1887

All change

Life in Britain changed a lot during Victorian times. One of the main reasons for this was the rise in manufacturing. Factories grew up all over the country and produced more goods than ever before. Britain became known as the 'workshop of the world' as it sold its products abroad. This was all part of the **Industrial Revolution**, a time of progress that made Britain very rich.

Look out for Sherlock's paw-prints – each one has a mystery for you to solve. The answers are on pages 30–31.

▲ Britain controlled many other countries in Victorian times. The British Empire in 1886 is shaded orange on this map.

Time to investigate!

In this book we are going to find out what it was like to work in a Victorian factory. At the end there is a project for you to complete. The history detective Sherlock Bones will help you by suggesting where to look for clues. Do not miss his 'Detective work' boxes and the list of websites on page 31.

Detective work

Look in libraries for books about the Victorians. Ask your relatives if they have any old photographs of workers from this time.

Working in factories

▲ Women work in a Lancashire cotton mill in 1897.

▼ Early factories were powered by waterwheels.

The invention of factories changed the way everyday items were made. People used to create things by hand, in small workshops or at home. This was slow and often expensive. Machines could produce more goods quickly, and at a cheaper price.

A matter of power

The earliest factories were set up in the mid-1700s to make textiles, such as cotton. They had to be built near rivers because they relied on water power. Victorian factories introduced steam power, produced by burning coal. Steam power could be used more widely and was able to drive much bigger and faster machines.

▲ *A mother and son spin wool by hand.*

'A steam engine with the strength of 880 men can work 50,000 spindles. All this needs only 750 workers to make as much yarn as 200,000 men did before.'

A Victorian manufacturer

Detective work

Find out about Victorian factories in your area. Discover what they produced, who owned them and how many people worked there. Kelly's Business Directories are useful for this – look in libraries or on the Internet.

Loom and gloom

Victorian factories forced many skilled workers out of business. Spinners and weavers were among the first to suffer. Their **hand looms** and spinning wheels could not keep up with speedy new cloth-makers like the **flying shuttle** and **spinning jenny**.

Factory attacks

Some craftsmen tried to stop the spread of factories by smashing the machines. But these attacks soon died out. Bit by bit, people began to accept that factories were the future.

❀ What are the rioters in the picture going to use to destroy the factory?

▼ *Mobs that attacked factories were called 'Luddites' after one of their leaders, Ned Ludd.*

Where did the workers live?

Extract from *Mary Barton*, written in 1848 by Elizabeth Gaskell:

'Three or four children were rolling on the damp...wet, brick floor, through which the stagnant, filthy moisture of the street oozed up; the fire-place was empty and black.'

Before Victorian times, most people lived and worked in the countryside. But as factories became more widespread, new towns and cities appeared. Existing towns grew bigger as people arrived from villages to find work.

▲ *Builders packed as many houses as possible into slum areas like this.*

In the slums

By the end of Queen Victoria's reign, most people lived in towns and cities. Factory workers lived mainly in poor **slum** areas. Here, badly built homes were crammed around dark courtyards linked by narrow streets.

Dirt and disease

Many families ate, bathed and slept together in one room. They had to fetch water from shared wells or pumps. Sewage and factory chemicals polluted the water. Rotting rubbish in the streets attracted rats.

Disease spread quickly in the dirty, cramped conditions. **Epidemics** of **cholera** and **typhoid** killed many people. In 1861, Queen Victoria's husband, Prince Albert, died of typhoid. The government reacted by passing new laws. They reduced overcrowding and upgraded water supplies, sewage systems and rubbish collection. Gradually, living conditions improved.

▼ *People were shocked when Prince Albert died of typhoid.*

▲ *This cartoon shows Death pouring water from a polluted pump.*

✿ What did this cartoon warn Victorian people about?

Detective work

Look on the Internet and in libraries for more information about Victorian towns. How are things different today?

What was factory work like?

The move to factories changed many people's working lives. In the countryside they followed daylight hours, working for longer in summer than in winter. They could take rests and chat or sing to pass the time. Factory life was very different.

Strict shifts

Factory owners made people work in shifts. Everyone on a shift had to start and finish at the same time every day. Some people worked at night and slept during the day. For the first time, they had to run their lives by the clock, rather than the Sun.

▼ Workers head home after a long factory shift.

Dull days

Factory life was boring and exhausting. Workers had to do the same thing day after day. They saw only a small part of what was being made, rather than creating it from start to finish. They also had to keep up with the machines.

Tough treatment

Many people, including children, worked 15-hour days with only short breaks for meals. If they were late, lazy, wasted materials or even whistled, they were punished. **Overseers** bullied and beat people who broke the rules, or took money from their pay.

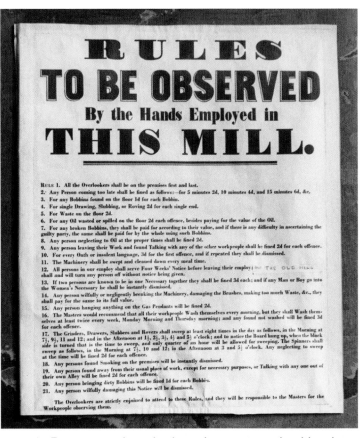

▲ *Factory workers had to obey strict rules like these.*

Detective work

Government officials sometimes interviewed factory workers. Search online for copies of their reports.

◀ *Children were beaten to keep them awake.*

❧ How would you feel after a 15-hour factory shift?

How safe were Victorian factories?

In early Victorian times, there were no laws about health and safety. Accidents in factories were common, and often deadly.

▲ Factory workers lost money if their machines were stopped. In this picture a child is cleaning under a working loom (on the right).

Risky machines

Factory machinery was dangerous to use. Workers could be caught in it by their hair or clothing. Children who cleaned the machines were at risk from the moving parts. It took years before safety guards were installed to protect people.

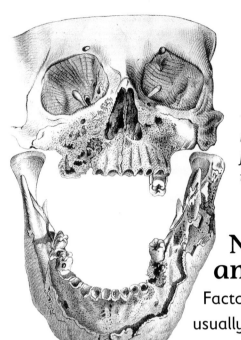

◀ *Phosphorous rotted people's jaws until their teeth fell out.*

Noise and fumes

Factories were usually dark, stuffy and very hot. The machine noise was deafening, and dust and fumes filled the air. Chemicals in some factories damaged people's health. Workers who made matches, for example, were poisoned by phosphorous which ate away the bones in their jaws.

No protection

Factory workers received no help if they were hurt or made ill by work. If they took time off, they were not paid. Those who could never work again relied on their families for support. Some were forced to beg. Others ended up in prison-like **workhouses** where they could eat and sleep in return for jobs.

Detective work

Charles Dickens was a Victorian writer who worked in a factory as a child. He also visited factories to research his stories. See what you can find out about his experience.

▲ *Charles Dickens wrote about Victorian factory life.*

'Cotton spinners work in a heat of 80–84°F [27–29°C]. They are locked in, except for half an hour at tea-time. Then there is the dust and fuzz, which they breathe in. Men are aged by it; they cannot work after 50 years of age. Children are deformed and made ill.'

William Cobbett, a Victorian **reformer**

Why did women and children work in factories?

Women and children were cheap for factory owners to employ. Victorian women earned half as much as men in the same jobs. Children were paid even less.

Orphan apprentices

Some factories used orphans as **apprentices**. They earned nothing except food and a bed – and usually these were gruesome. Apprentices were given the worst jobs, and the worst treatment. They had no one to turn to for protection.

Apprentices who were caught running away were beaten. At night, they were locked in a dark room with only a blanket to sleep on.

▲ *Women work in a pen factory in 1851.*

✿ Why do you think women were chosen to make things like pen nibs?

◀ *Children's wages were rarely enough to buy shoes.*

▲ *The women in this factory had a lunch hour —
in many factories this was not the case.*

New laws

Eventually, laws were passed to protect
women and children in factories. In 1850,
their working day was limited to ten hours.
Other laws led to better treatment and even
some schooling for apprentices.

New lifestyle

As factory life improved, some women began
to enjoy it. They made friends and earned
money. In many areas where women had
no time to cook at home, services such as
fish and chip shops were set up.

*'My girls work, I can find none. When
the mills are busy they work from three
in the morning 'til ten or half past ten
at night…When they get home they
are so tired that they fall asleep with
their supper still in their mouths.'*

Father of two girls working in a
cotton mill

Detective work

Compare your school day with a child
factory worker's. Investigate life in
different factories using the Internet.

How did factory life get better?

As Queen Victoria's reign went on, well-off people became more aware of the tough lives of the poor. Some became reformers, who went round persuading people that things needed to improve.

Reforming the rules

Many reformers felt they had a Christian duty to help people worse-off than themselves. The Earl of Shaftesbury was one of them. His reports on factories and mines encouraged politicians to make new laws. At first, many factory owners ignored the laws that protected their workers. Then the government sent inspectors to check up on them. Gradually, employers were forced to obey the rules.

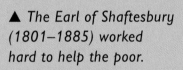

▲ The Earl of Shaftesbury (1801–1885) worked hard to help the poor.

▶ Inspectors took evidence from workers, like these children, about factory conditions.

✤ Do you think the children would tell the truth with their overseer listening in the background?

▲ *The artist Robert Cruikshank drew attention to child workers through cartoons like this.*

▶ *Sir Edwin Chadwick helped to improve public health.*

Improving homes

Sir Edwin Chadwick was another Victorian reformer. In 1842, he wrote a book that shocked people with stories of the slums. It led to new efforts to clean up the streets and install proper water supplies.

Words and action

Newspaper editors and journalists joined the reformers, as did authors such as Charles Dickens. Their writings spread the word about factory and slum conditions, and helped to bring about change. By the end of Victoria's reign, workers had a much easier life than they did at the beginning.

Charles Dickens describes a Victorian factory town in his book *Hard Times:*

'It was a town of machinery and tall chimneys…It had a black canal in it, and a river that ran purple with ill-smelling dye, and vast piles of buildings full of windows where there was a rattling and a trembling all day long…'

Workers protest

Factories employed so many people that it was easy for workers to get together and protest. They formed groups called **trade unions** to fight for better pay and working conditions. There were different trade unions for different types of job.

Refusing to work

One of the main tactics used by trade unions was striking. During a strike, union members refused to work until they got what they wanted. They formed large crowds, or **pickets**, at the factory gates to persuade other workers to stay away, too.

Detective work

Were there strikes in your area in Victorian times? Find out about local trade unions at their offices, in libraries or online.

✿ Whose side do you think this illustrator was on?

▼ *Police try to stop a protest by match workers in 1871.*

▲ *Match workers protest against their treatment by factories and the police.*

Picket fights

Factory owners needed their workers to be in the right place at the right time. When a strike was called, they sometimes hired other workers to take over. Police or soldiers came in to break up the pickets. This often led to injuries on both sides.

The right to strike

Strikes and pickets were illegal at first, and cost many people their jobs. But as the workers gained public sympathy, they were given the right to strike. Bosses came to realise that it was better to talk with the unions than be faced with a costly picket.

The Royal Commission Report on Trade Unions stated:

'The objects of trade unions are in general of a twofold character –
First:...to afford relief to members of the union incapacitated from work [unable to work] *by accident or sickness; to allow a sum for the funeral expenses of members and their wives. Secondly:...to watch over and promote the interests of the working classes – and especially to protect them against undue advantage which the command of a large capital is supposed by them to give to the employers of labour.'*

What was a friendly society?

Victorians who fell on hard times received very little help from the government. They had to find other ways to protect themselves when money was short. Many better-paid workers joined friendly societies. These charged a weekly fee in return for payouts if a person became ill or unemployed.

Creating the Co-op

Food and other essentials took up most of a factory worker's wage. In 1844, a group of weavers in Rochdale set up a shop selling quality goods at a fair price. Customers could join the **co-operative** that ran the shop and receive a share of the profits. Soon there were Co-op shops all over the country – and they still work in the same way today.

✿ What could people buy from the Co-op below?

Detective work

Write to your local Co-op head office to find out if there was a branch in your area in Victorian times.

▼ *A Co-op store in late-Victorian London.*

◀ *Chartists meet on Kennington Common, London in 1848.*

Extract from a Chartist announcement:

'Government was designed to protect the freedom and promote the happiness of…the whole people…Any form of government which fails…ought to be amended or resisted.'

The right to vote

In 1837, only wealthy men could vote in elections or sit in Parliament. This meant that laws rarely favoured working people. Groups known as **Chartists** started to protest and demand the right for all men to vote.

▼ *An election poster for Keir Hardie promises improvements for poor workers.*

Many workers supported the Chartists, and in 1867 they finally achieved their aim. In 1892, the people elected Keir Hardie, the first **socialist** member of parliament. The following year, the Independent Labour Party was formed. Slowly, the government began to pay more attention to the needs of the poor.

VOTE FOR

Home Rule.

Democratic Government.

Justice to Labour

No Monopoly.

No Landlordism

Temperance Reform.

Healthy Homes.

Fair Rents.

Eight-Hour Day.

Work for the Unemployed.

KEIR HARDIE.

Printed and Published by F. W. Scu se & Co. [L.S.C.], 151, Barking Road, Canning Town, London, E.

Were all bosses bad?

◀ *Robert Owen (left) owned cotton mills in New Lanark, Scotland (above).*

Factory owners became richer during Victorian times. Some built huge country **estates** and lived far away from the dirty towns. Many bosses were interested only in making money and did little to look after their workers. But others were more caring.

Robert Owen

Robert Owen was a Scottish mill owner. He paid his employees good wages and cut down their working hours. He also gave them decent housing, ran a school for the children and refused to employ anyone under ten years old.

🐾 Do you think the artist of the portrait on the left thought Owen was a good or bad boss?

Salt, Lever and Cadbury

In 1853, a factory owner called Titus Salt founded the workers' village of Saltaire, near Bradford. This was a light, airy factory surrounded by comfortable new homes. In 1888, soap maker William Lever built Port Sunlight, a similar scheme in Merseyside. George Cadbury set up the 'model village' of Bournville in 1893, for workers at his Birmingham chocolate factory.

Happy and hard-working

Factory bosses slowly began to realise that people worked better if they were happy and healthy. By the end of Victoria's reign, employers were arranging regular social events and outings for their staff.

> *'It does not appear to me necessary for children to be employed under ten years of age in any regular work. I instruct them and give them exercise.'*
> Robert Owen

Detective work

Look up books and articles about the life of Robert Owen. Can you see why he was such a kind boss?

▼ *Victorian workers enjoy an outing to the seaside.*

Where did Victorians go shopping?

Detective work

Look in museums for Victorian products, packaging and advertisements. Search the 24-Hour Museum website (see page 31) to find a collection near you.

Victorian factories helped to make Britain one of the richest countries in the world. Shopping became an increasingly popular pastime as shelves were stacked with new and exciting things to buy.

'Shop till you drop could have been coined in the nineteenth century when it seemed that anything could be bought...Food, fashion and furnishings, books, toys and beauty preparations – the Victorian shopper wanted them all.'
Modern historian, Maurice Barren in 1998

▼ Victorians loved department stores like this one in Edinburgh.

◄ *People began to live in more comfortable surroundings as their pay improved and workers had more rights.*

New comforts

As wages rose and factory-made products became cheaper, life improved for most Victorians. Some became part of a new **middle class** who owned many luxury goods and gadgets. Even poor workers could afford more comforts than they had before.

Under one roof

Victorians in towns and cities flocked to new department stores. Elegant indoor arcades sprang up too, allowing people to go from shop to shop within a pleasant covered area.

Colourful displays

The new variety of goods in the shops meant lots of competition between rival firms. All over town, there were posters advertising anything from hair oil to bicycles. Eye-catching packaging made products stand out on the shelves.

▶ *A Victorian poster advertises oil heaters.*

Wright & Butler's Oil Heating Stoves

The Great Exhibition

In 1851, a showcase of British manufacturing took place in London's Hyde Park. It was called the Great Exhibition. The idea came from a man called Henry Cole and was promoted by Queen Victoria's husband, Prince Albert.

▲ *The Great Exhibition aimed to show off British products and win new orders from abroad.*

The Crystal Palace

The exhibition was held in an iron-and-glass building called the Crystal Palace. It measured 600 metres long by 120 metres wide and contained 300,000 panes of glass. It was built in just 15 months using factory-made parts.

Detective work

Look for details about the Great Exhibition in pictures and articles online.

▶ *The Crystal Palace was designed by Joseph Paxton, especially for the Great Exhibition.*

'What used to be done by hand and used to take months is now done in a few instants by the most beautiful machinery.'

Queen Victoria at the Great Exhibition

◀ At the Great Exhibition, wealthy people got a chance to see factory machinery at work.

Drawing the crowds

In only 20 weeks, more than 6 million people visited the Great Exhibition. Some train and bus companies organised special trips. The crowds were wowed by an amazing display of manufactured goods, ranging from steam engines and factory machinery to tiny ornaments and toys. Unusual gadgets included a pocket knife with 80 blades and a bed that could tip people into a cold bath to wake them up!

Lasting impression

For many people, the Great Exhibition proved that Britain was the world's leading industrial nation. It was not long before countries such as Germany and the USA overtook. But no one can deny that Victorian factories played a vital part in shaping the modern world.

🐾 Do you think factory workers would have described the machinery as beautiful, like Queen Victoria did?

Your project

Are you ready to gather all your evidence on Victorian factories? If you have been doing your detective work, you should have found plenty of clues! This is where you can bring them to life and create your own original project.

One of these questions might help you to choose a good topic...

• What was it like to be a Victorian factory worker?
• Did Victorian factories have an impact in your area?
• How did Victorian manufacturing affect people's lives?
• Why was Victorian Britain called 'the workshop of the world'?
• How did factory life change during Victorian times?
• Were Victorian factories different from today's?

▼ Use the photos in this book to help you picture how Victorian workers lived.

Presentation ideas

Try to think of a fun way to present your project. Here are just a few ideas:

- Imagine you are a Victorian worker writing a diary about your daily life.
- Type up your evidence in the style of a Victorian newspaper.
- Make a poster for a Victorian manufacturing company, advertising how their products could improve people's lives.
- Pretend to be a factory inspector reporting on poor working conditions or a cruel factory boss.

▲▼ Can you put yourself in the place of one of these shoe makers (above) or matchstick sellers (below)?

Detective debate

You could work with a friend to present two sides of an argument. For example, some Victorians thought that children should work in factories. How would they debate this with others who disagreed?

Glossary

apprentice A trainee worker who by law has to stay in the job for a set length of time.

Chartists Victorians who campaigned for political change.

cholera An infectious disease, usually caused by contaminated water or food.

epidemic An outbreak of disease.

estate A large property, including land and buildings.

flying shuttle A fast Victorian weaving machine.

hand loom A device used to weave fabric by hand.

Industrial Revolution The period from the late 1700s to the early 1800s when factories developed and work became more concentrated in towns than in the country.

middle class A social class of people who can afford to live comfortably.

overseer Someone who makes sure people do their jobs properly.

pickets Protestors who try to persuade others not to work during a strike.

reformers People who campaign for change.

slum A neighbourhood with unhealthy, overcrowded living conditions.

socialist Believing in collective ownership of businesses and equal wealth for all.

spinning jenny A Victorian machine that spun wool into thread, invented by James Hargreaves.

trade union An organisation that looks after workers' rights.

typhoid An infectious disease, usually caused by contaminated water or food.

workhouse A poorhouse where people worked for food and a bed.

Answers

page 7

The rioters are going to destroy the factory using axes and flames.

page 9

The cartoon warned people of the need for clean water supplies to prevent the spread of deadly diseases.

page 11

A 15-hour factory shift would be exhausting. You would probably just want to sleep.

page 14

Women were given delicate work because they had smaller hands and nimbler fingers than men.

page 16

With an overseer watching, children may have been too afraid to say bad things about the factory in case they got punished.

page 18

You can tell the illustrator supported the protestors because the police are shown threatening the women and children.

page 20

The shop sign suggests a range of goods including meat, groceries, fabrics [drapery] and stockings [hosiery].

page 22

✽ The artist has made Robert Owen look important but kind – a good boss.

page 27

✽ People who worked long hours or were injured in the factories probably wouldn't have described the machines as beautiful.

Books to read

At Work (A Victorian Childhood) by Ruth Thomson (Franklin Watts, 2007)

Victorian Workhouse (My Story) by Pamela Oldfield (Scholastic, 2004)

Mill Girl (My Story) by Pamela Oldfield (Scholastic, 2008)

Victorians (Eyewitness) by Ann Kramer (Dorling Kindersley, 2008)

Victorian Britain (Life in the Past) by Mandy Ross (Heinemann Library, 2006)

Places to visit

Armley Mills Industrial Museum, Leeds
www.leeds.gov.uk/ArmleyMills

Blists Hill Victorian Town, Telford, Shropshire
www.ironbridge.org.uk/our_attractions/blists_hill_victorian_town

Bradford Industrial Museum and Horses at Work, West Yorkshire
www.bradfordmuseums.org/industrialmuseum/index.htm

Long Shop Museum, Leiston, Suffolk
www.longshop.care4free.net

New Lanark Visitor Centre, South Lanarkshire, Scotland
www.newlanark.org

Useful websites

www.24hourmuseum.org.uk/index.html
Find out about museums and exhibitions near you, or take part in an online trail.

www.learningcurve.gov.uk/index/keystage2.htm
Scroll down to the Victorian sections and click on a topic that interests you.

www.schoolhistory.co.uk
Type 'Victorian' into the search box and follow the links.

www.victorians.org.uk
Investigate lots of Victorian evidence, including a factory logbook.

Index

Numbers in **bold** refer to pictures